MW01519619

LIFE AFTER
LOSING A
LOVED
ONE

LIFE AFTER LOSING A LOVED ONE

BY

TIARA DIONNE

LEARN HOW TO LIVE AGAIN AFTER LOSING A LOVED ONE

Life After Losing A Loved One
Tiara Dionne

All rights reserved
First Edition, 2021
© Tiara Dionne, 2021

No part of this publication may be reproduced, or stored
in a retrieval system, or transmitted in any form by means
of electronic, mechanical, photocopying or otherwise,
without prior written permission from the author.

Life After a Losing a Loved One

Where do I find the words? There are never the right words to say after a death. When it is someone dear to you, someone you know, someone you love...it shocks your soul in a way that you cannot even imagine.

Often, when a person we love has passed away we find ourselves going through a lot of motions. We feel empty, lost, we lose sleep, we lose touch with reality, and we begin to question life, God, and the entirety of everything that has existed.

When my aunt passed, I felt like someone shot me in my chest. I never saw it coming, (at least not so soon, not so fast). I cried so much my tears could have become a river. I wanted her back. I wanted the news to not be true.

The more I processed that she had been in a car accident and died instantly, the more I found myself denying what happened. It didn't seem possible that something so tragic could happen to someone I loved so much. Picturing what she had gone though was unbearable to imagine.

It didn't help that it was on the news, and I refused to watch it and allow the words of the tragedy repeat over and over. Losing her was enough and shortly after I found out that my baby cousin, 18 months old, was in the car as well and was in critical condition.

I never saw the day coming when I would need to attend a funeral for two. In the end, he didn't survive either. How could this be possible to mourn two deaths at once?

There is a reason why I made moving past trauma my mission in my business because it's so easy to stay in that place of hurt. The vision of my small business is to help women move past trauma while finding purpose. But what do you do when you been given a dose of your own medicine?

Truthfully, it's always much easier from the outside looking in, but having experienced it all first hand. I can tell you *exactly* how to get through.

We are each given specific experiences and situations to use what we have been through to remind others that it is possible to face trauma head-on and still find purpose.

I have lost close friends and family over the years. I have been through depression and battled a tumor. However, every traumatic experience is different.

I had to find the courage to put on my hat, my armor, that said,

"You are valuable, you are born with a purpose, you are here on an assignment."

After I put on that hat, I said the words as well to myself over and over again. Until it sank into my soul.

My purpose with this book is to help you find *you* again. To help you begin to live life after a loss.

No one knows the day or the hour that anyone will leave this earth. That's the scary part but we are not meant to live in fear.

STAGES OF GRIEVING

The most common reactions/stages to loss are:
* denial
* anger
* bargaining
* depression
* acceptance

There's no way to avoid the stages of grief - they are very real. You may experience one or more than one, but the fact is you will find yourself experiencing these emotions.

Keep in mind, that you are in control of your time and that no one else, including your place of employment, can rush you or invalidate your feelings. Your feelings and your state of health matter more. Be advised, and take the time you need. What good would you be to people if you are no good to yourself?

Some tips to consider. As a piece of homework let your job know or clients know what's going on so you can take the time you need for you. Reflect on finances. It's always good to have emergency money saved for all types of situations including traveling and funeral expenses. If you have money saved, take some time away.

Let yourself feel the emotions.
If you need to cry - allow yourself to cry, there's a lot of healing in your tears. Holding back just harbors your heart. Let it flow if you need to. You may feel things you never thought you would feel. You may realize that seeing a picture, tv show, different smells, foods, objects, and even certain people can be a "trigger."

An emotional trigger is anything — including memories, experiences, or events — that sparks an intense emotional reaction regardless of your current mood. Emotional triggers are associated with post-traumatic stress disorder (PTSD). (https://www.healthline.com/health/mental-health/emotional-triggers)

What can you do?
Take each day and each moment one step at a time, and of all try your hardest to face how you feel.

When I first arrived at my aunt's house after she passed, I felt angry. I couldn't even cry. I just was beyond upset. I kept feeling in denial. I believed that she was just going to drive up and hop out of the car but she didn't. As I walked into her house I began to feel even angrier than when I was just sitting outside of the house in the car.

Shock, denial, and anger felt like they were happening all at once. Remind yourself, it is normal. Keep allowing your emotions to pour through you.

An exercise that may help:
First, have a tissue nearby. This next exercise may be an emotional one, but it will help you start to practice accepting your feelings.

Write everything you are currently feeling down. Every thought that comes to mind about your loved one who has passed. Write it down. Take this time to reflect, hear your thoughts, and to take the time you need.

....

....

....

....

....

....

....

....

....

....

....

....

....

....

....

Life After Losing A Loved One

....

....

....

....

....

....

....

....

....

....

....

....

....

....

....

....

....

....

....

....

....

....

....

....

....

....

....

....

....

....

....

....

....

....

....

....

....

....

....

....

....

....
....
....
....
....
....
....
....
....
....
....
....
....
....
....
....
....
....
....
....
....
....

Please don't move on until you have written something down. This is a huge part of the process. If you feel you have nothing to write. Reflect on: How your loved one would want you to move forward. Then, take a break and come back when you do have something to write, even if it's not in response to the prompt, but it helped bring on other thoughts.

Now that you have had a chance to write something down. Share.. Say out loud how you feel. Before you say it aloud, take at least three deep breaths.

You got this!

Now, for the last part.

Write down 3 things that bring you joy. This may be hard but it will be a great tool for the long run.

Writhing down the things that bring you joy allow you to always have a core value. This means that no matter what if you are angry, sad, mad, feeling hopeless, etc. You will choose one of the three tools that you know will bring you joy.

Only you know what can make you happy. 💡 Think about tangible things. Things that are easily accessible, that no matter what, when your feeling sad or down, "that thing" will be available during your time of need.

List the three items below that bring you joy, & please do not move on until this step is complete:

....
....
....
....
....
....
....
....
....
....
....
....
....
....
....
....
....
....
....
....

....

....

....

....

....

....

....

....

....

....

....

....

....

....

....

....

....

....

....

....

....

....
....
....
....
....
....
....
....
....
....
....
....
....
....
....
....
....
....
....
....
....
....

Your New Reality

Coming to terms with your new reality will be hard. Some days you will feel motivated, some days you will not. Sometimes you may just break down and cry out of no where, and other times you will keep your composure.

Own your grieving process. It is your own! No one else can tell you how fast or how you should grieve. Even when it comes to this manual, this is simply support, guidance, and the goal is to point you in the right direction for you to understand when to choose joy. Happiness is a choose, and while we may be sad, we have to keep in mind that it's ok to not be ok, but we cannot stay there.

Choosing joy over sadness daily is a power. It is a power we all have in us that has to be activated. We never know that power until we are in that moment of wanting to be sad and choosing what we know will bring us joy.

Let joy be the light in a dark place when you need it. What better way to gain control to begin living your life again by making a decision to start your day with joy intentionally.

It is so easy to allow darkness and depression to sneak up, especially when the funeral ends and everyone has gone back to their own lives & homes. However, changing the frequency to live life after a loss is key! We cannot go back to how things used to be. Frequency is repetition, and the second we start doing something different then the old way, a new pattern has to begin.

We can literally change the course of our journey by being proactive about making sure to not go back to how things used to be, but creating new life, new objectives, even a new mindset.

Discovering who you are and what your mission is, is everything! Sometimes we get so close to someone, we lose sight of ourselves, our wants, our desires. On the other hand, we may have found that our loved one came, brought purpose, and meaning to our lives and that is a gift we will always have in our hearts.

But that could have been their purpose for the connection to help you see that they bring life, a life of meaning. A life that is more than just working your 9 to 5, paying bills, and dying.

"There's something about death that teaches us about life."

We either learn to appreciate life more, we start something new, find purpose, or sadly, we go back to the old patterns.

What will you do?
No one has the answer other than you and God.

While finding your rhythm aside from how things used to be, it is imperative to practice how to move forward and learn how to focus less on the past by creating new memories. Allowing yourself to choose joy, despite the uncertainty is faith. I dare you to do something different. I encourage you to begin to open your heart and mind to giving in to what could become your best self.

Here's a little homework that may ignite stepping outside of your comfort zone. I want you to choose one of the following to do. These are tools that can help you get the help you may need:

- [ ] **google local support groups for families who experience loss**
- [ ] **get connected with Facebook groups or someone you can trust**
- [ ] **journal, paint, draw, listen to music, take a walk, go out to eat with friends, do something fun etc.**

Start incorporating something that will allow you to give yourself some personal time to reflect and remind you that you are alive and can still enjoy things too.

Be open, give yourself the time you need, and allow people to help you; whether it's cooking, cleaning, bringing you food. Of all the advice I can give the most important is, *stay connected.*

You got this!

Constantly reflect on your feelings because they matter. Your mental health and overall wellness is everything. If you are feeling depressed (really sad, lack of motivation, suicidal thoughts) please please please get help! It's normal to experience extreme sadness, but it is not okay to stay there. Some things we cannot face on our own. Don't let embarrassment get in the way of asking for help. Your life matters.

Remember healing takes time, and there is no right or wrong way to grieve. Moving forward can take a month, or several years but remember, this is all determined by you.

When I finally started healing I remember thinking wow I never thought I'd get through this, but I chose myself. Choose you daily. Choose joy. Choose what will make YOU happy.

If I can find my way through these dark waters and find purpose amidst loss I know you can too.

My condolences to you & your family. I'm thinking of you & I've praying for every reader who purchased or was gifted this book. My heart goes out to you.

I see you, I love you, & you are not alone!

Made in the USA
Middletown, DE
30 August 2023

37618799R00015